W9-ASC-189

If you were a
TIMES
SIGN

by Trisha Speed Shaskan
illustrated by Sarah Dillard

PICTURE WINDOW BOOKS
Minneapolis, Minnesota

times sign (x) a symbol used to show multiplication

Editors: Christianne Jones and Jill Kalz
Designer: Lori Bye
Page Production: Melissa Kes
Art Director: Nathan Gassman
Editorial Director: Nick Healy
The illustrations in this book were created with watercolor
and gouache.

Picture Window Books
151 Good Counsel Drive, P.O. Box 669
Mankato, MN 56002-0669
877-845-8392
www.capstonepub.com

Printed in the United States of America in North Mankato, MN.
062010   005856R

Library of Congress Cataloging-in-Publication Data
Shaskan, Trisha Speed, 1973–
If you were a times sign / by Trisha Speed Shaskan ;
illustrated by Sarah Dillard.
p. cm. — (Math Fun)
Includes index.
ISBN 978-1-4048-5210-5 (library binding)
ISBN 978-1-4048-5211-2 (paperback)
1. Multiplication—Juvenile literature. 2. Mathematical
notation—Juvenile literature. I. Dillard, Sarah, 1961- ill. II. Title.
QC115.S5265 2009
513.2'13—dc22
                                    2008037913

Special thanks to our adviser for his expertise:

Stuart Farm, M.Ed., Mathematics Lecturer
University of North Dakota

If you were a times sign ...

... you would multiply one number by another number.

Shelly sails ashore with four six-packs of soda cans.

Four times six equals twenty-four soda cans.

$$4 \times 6 = 24$$

$$\begin{array}{r} 4 \\ \times\ 6 \\ \hline 24 \end{array}$$

If you were a times sign, you would be a symbol used to show multiplication. Multiplication is a quick way to add the same number over and over.

Five diving dragonflies have six legs each. Five dragonflies times six legs each equals thirty legs in all.

$5 \times 6 = 30$

$6+6+6+6+6=30$

Five sneaky spiders have eight legs each. Five spiders times eight legs each equals forty legs in all.

$$5 \times 8 = 40$$

$$8+8+8+8+8=40$$

If you were a times sign, you would be part of a multiplication problem. The problem's answer is called the product.

Ribbon snakes have three white stripes on their backs. Three ribbon snakes times three white stripes each equals nine white stripes total. The product is nine.

$$3 \times 3 = 9$$

Two mice race on each white stripe. Two mice times nine stripes equals eighteen mice total. The product is eighteen.

$$2 \times 9 = 18$$

If you were a times sign, you could switch the number before you and the number after you. It wouldn't matter which number came first because the product would be the same.

$$2 \times 3 = 6$$

Two tigers' tricycles have three wheels each. Two tricycles times three wheels each equals six wheels total.

Three bears' bicycles have two wheels each.
Three bicycles times two wheels each
equals six wheels total.

$$3 \times 2 = 6$$

If you were a times sign, you could work left to right or top to bottom.

Toucan has two toasters.
Each toaster holds four pieces of bread.
Toucan fills the two toasters.

Two toasters times four pieces of bread each equals eight pieces of bread in all.

2☒4=8

Toucan takes the toast to the twins.
Two plates times four pieces of toast
on each equals eight pieces of toast in all.

$$\begin{array}{r} 2 \\ \times\,4 \\ \hline 8 \end{array}$$

If you were a times sign, you could be used like the words "groups of."

Fifi holds two groups of five balloons.
Two groups of five equals ten balloons.

$$2 \times 5 = 10$$

$$\begin{array}{r} 2 \\ \times 5 \\ \hline 10 \end{array}$$

$$4 \times 5 = 20$$

Fifi flies away with four groups of five balloons.
Four groups of five equals twenty balloons.

If you were a times sign, you could be part of a story problem.

Each day the kangaroos play basketball.
On Friday, Caleb scored four baskets.
Each basket was worth two points.
Kate scored three three-pointers.
Who scored the most points?

Hint:
Caleb's score would be the product of **4**✗**2**.
Kate's score would be the product of **3**✗**3**.

Answer: Caleb scored 8 points, and Kate scored 9.

17

If you were a times sign, you would be the opposite of a divided-by sign. Multiplication uses repeated addition. Division uses repeated subtraction.

Three octopuses wear flippers
on the ends of their arms.
Three octopuses times eight arms
each equals twenty-four flippers.

$$8+8+8=24$$

$$3 \times 8 = 24$$

Suddenly, the flippers slip off! Twenty-four lost flippers divided by eight empty arms on each octopus equals three sad octopuses.

$$24 \div 8 = 3$$

$$24 - 8 - 8 - 8 = 0$$

If you were a times sign, you could multiply single-digit or double-digit numbers.

Two seven-eyed aliens land on Saturn. Two aliens times seven eyes each equals fourteen eyes total.

$$2 \times 7 = 14$$

Ten ten-eyed aliens greet them.
Ten aliens times ten eyes each
equals 100 eyes total.

$$\begin{array}{r} 10 \\ \times 10 \\ \hline 100 \end{array}$$

You would always multiply ...

Multiplication Table

X	0	1	2	3	4	5	6	7	8	9	10
0	0	0	0	0	0	0	0	0	0	0	0
1	0	1	2	3	4	5	6	7	8	9	10
2	0	2	4	6	8	10	12	14	16	18	20
3	0	3	6	9	12	15	18	21	24	27	30
4	0	4	8	12	16	20	24	28	32	36	40
5	0	5	10	15	20	25	30	35	40	45	50
6	0	6	12	18	24	30	36	42	48	54	60
7	0	7	14	21	28	35	42	49	56	63	70
8	0	8	16	24	32	40	48	56	64	72	80
9	0	9	18	27	36	45	54	63	72	81	90
10	0	10	20	30	40	50	60	70	80	90	100

... if you were a times sign.

MULTIPLICATION FUN

What you need:

an empty egg carton   a pen or pencil

50 pennies   a piece of paper

What you do:

1. Fill six of the cups in the egg carton with two pennies each.
2. Count the number of pennies. The total is the product of 6x2.
3. Fill six of the cups in the carton with three pennies each. Count the number of pennies. The total is the product of 6x3.
4. Create your own multiplication problems. For example, fill some of the cups with four pennies each. Be sure to use the same number of pennies in each cup. If you fill one cup with two pennies, fill them all with two pennies. Multiplication is just repeated addition!
5. List the multiplication problems and the products you come up with on a piece of paper. Use the multiplication table on page 22 to check your answers!

Glossary

digit—any of the numbers 1 through 9, and sometimes 0

divided-by sign—a symbol used to show division

division—a quick way to repeatedly subtract the same number

multiplication—a quick way to repeatedly add the same number

product—the number found from multiplying two or more numbers

symbol—a sign that stands for something to be done

times sign—a symbol used to show multiplication

Index

To Learn More

More Books to Read

Chrismer, Melanie. *Multiply This!* New York: Children's Press, 2005.

Freeman, Marcia S. *Multiply by Hand: The Nines Facts.* Vero Beach, Fla.: Rourke Pub., 2008.

On the Web

FactHound offers a safe, fun way to find educator-approved Internet sites related to this book.

Here's what you do:

1. Visit *www.facthound.com*
2. Choose your grade level.
3. Begin your search.

This book's ID number is 9781404852105

Look for all of the books in the Math Fun series:

If You Were a Divided-by Sign

If You Were a Fraction

If You Were a Minus Sign

If You Were a Minute

If You Were a Plus Sign

If You Were a Pound or a Kilogram

If You Were a Quart or a Liter

If You Were a Set

If You Were a Times Sign

If You Were an Even Number

If You Were an Inch or a Centimeter

If You Were an Odd Number